Mystery
MONSTERS
of
Loch Ness

For years the Loch Ness monster was treated as a joke. But now some scientists think there is indeed something in the loch—a colony of very large animals of some kind. What could they be?

The author handles this intriguing question as an ecology mystery. She lays out the evidence and considers the loch as an environment for animal life. She then surveys the animal kingdom to discover which of its members might be able to live in the loch and might also fit the description of the monsters. Young readers will enjoy trying to solve the mystery, and along the way they will learn a surprising amount of science.

MYSTERY MONSTERS OF LOCH NESS

By Patricia Lauber

GARRARD PUBLISHING COMPANY

CHAMPAIGN, ILLINOIS

Photo credits:

©Academy of Applied Science, Boston: pp. 6, 19, 20-21 (all)

American Museum of Natural History: pp. 36, 40 (top), 47

Associated Newspapers Group, London/Photo Researchers: pp. 2, 15 (bottom)

Bettmann Archive: p. 9

Field Museum of Natural History, Chicago: p. 37 (both)

Fritz Henle/Photo Researchers: p. 31

D. Hughes/Bruce Coleman, Inc.: p. 44

Russ Kinne/Photo Researchers: p. 40 (bottom)

Tom McHugh/Photo Researchers: pp. 52 (top), 61 (right)

National Film Archive, London: p. 22

Photo Trends: p. 15 (top)

Pictorial Parade: p. 16

Alvin E. Staffan/Photo Researchers: pp. 52 (bottom), 61 (left)

Library of Congress Cataloging in Publication Data

Lauber, Patricia.
  Mystery monsters of Loch Ness.

  Includes index.
  SUMMARY: Discusses several theories about the identity and origin of the Loch Ness monster.
  1. Loch Ness monster—Juvenile literature.
[1. Loch Ness monster. 2. Monsters] I. Title.
QL89.2.L6L38   001.9'44   77-13913
ISBN 0-8116-6109-1

Cover, map, and drawings

by Victor Mays

CONTENTS

1. Monsters in the Loch? 7

2. Where Did They Come From? . 23

3. The Loch as a Home 29

4. What Could They Be? 35

5. What Else Could They Be? . . . 49

Mystery monsters
might look something like this.

1. Monsters in the Loch?

In the north of Scotland, there is a long, narrow lake. Mountains rise along its sides. Between them, the big lake stretches as far as the eye can see. The water is deep and dark. This is Loch Ness—*loch* is the Scottish word for "lake."

Loch Ness is a lake with a mystery. The mystery goes back hundreds of years. It has to do with a big, strange creature that was said to live in the loch.

Local people believed in this creature. They spoke of it as "the beastie in the loch." Most of the time, they said, the beastie lived underwater. But once in a while it came to the surface. Then someone might catch sight of its head or its back or its tail. What was it? No one could say, for no one ever got a good look at it. They thought it must be some kind of fish, since it lived in the loch. But it did not look like any fish they knew.

Before the 1930s, few outsiders had heard of the beastie. Then a road was built along Loch Ness. Many visitors began seeing the loch and hearing about the beastie. Some believed they had caught sight of it.

One of these sightings was written

For hundreds of years
people have talked and written
about huge, strange animals.
They told of sea serpents, such as
this one, and of dragons and giant worms
and water horses. Today it is hard to tell
which of these animals were real
and which were made up. But
it does seem sure that there
was something. One of these animals
seems to have lived in Loch Ness.
One account of it is 1,400 years old.

up for a local newspaper. When the editor read the story, he said, "If it's that big, we'll have to call it a monster." That was how the beastie in the loch became the Loch Ness monster. From then on, many papers printed stories about the monster. They made good reading.

These stories made the monster famous. But many readers thought it was a joke. To them, a monster was a make-believe animal, something they might see in a movie. They thought the Scots had invented a monster to draw tourists to the loch.

Accounts of the Loch Ness monster also sounded like jokes. Many people thought they had seen part of it. The parts added up to a very strange creature indeed.

It was said to be 20 or 30 or 50 feet long. The body was thick in the middle, but it thinned out toward the ends. There was a long neck with a small head. Some people had seen what looked like horns or feelers—two fleshy stalks that grew out of the head. Some had seen a stiff mane or fin on the neck and shoulders.

Sometimes the back looked like an overturned boat. At other times it had one, two, or three humps. Some people saw two or four flippers. They said the monster swam by paddling with its flippers. Other people saw no flippers. They said it swam by using its powerful tail.

The monster seemed shy. It never attacked boats or people. It was easily startled by noises, such as the slam of

A land sighting
was reported in July 1933
by Mr. and Mrs. George Spicer
of London, England.
They were driving
beside the loch when they
suddenly saw a thing coming
out of the bushes
some distance ahead.
It looked
like an elephant's trunk

but proved to be a long neck.
Behind it came a huge
gray body, 5 feet high
and 20 feet long.
Something was flapping at its neck.
Mr. Spicer thought this was
the creature's tail, which
it had curled out of the way.
Later the Spicers said
they felt they had been watching
something like a giant snail.

a car door or the putt-putt of an outboard motor. Any noise caused it to disappear. Sometimes the monster sank silently from sight. Sometimes it dived, churning up the water with its tail.

Some people thought the monster could climb out of the loch. A few claimed to have sighted it on land. Local people told of bent and broken bushes near the loch. They believed these were places where the monster had come out and lain down.

Was there ever such a creature? Could there be?

It doesn't sound likely. Yet some things are hard to explain if there is no monster.

Some sightings are very old. They were made long before the road was built and the monster became famous.

Some of the newer sightings were made by people who know the loch. These are men who have worked on or around it all their lives. They know what deer, otters, and logs look like in the loch. They know the strange waves that form. They know that on calm days the loch is like a mirror. It reflects clouds and birds, which may look like something in the loch.

These men can judge size and distance. If they see a long neck and a small head, they know whether they are looking at a fishing bird or at something else. They are not likely to make mistakes.

Photos are like the sightings. Most are probably of birds, otters, logs, or rocks. But a few do seem to show a large animal of some kind.

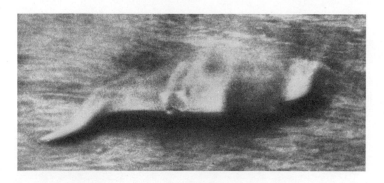

In November 1933 a man named Hugh Gray
took this photo from above Loch Ness.
He thought the neck was to the left and
that the head was underwater. The creature
seemed to be 20 to 30 feet long. If it
isn't the monster, what is it?

In April 1934 R. Kenneth Wilson,
a London surgeon, saw and photographed
a snakelike head, a long neck, and a hump.
He had no way to judge
the animal's size. Is this the monster?
Or is it a long-necked fishing bird?

Lachlan Stuart was a woodsman who lived
beside Loch Ness. Early one morning
in July 1951 he saw something moving
in the loch. At first he thought it was
a boat, but then he saw it had humps and
a long neck. He took this photo, which shows
only the humps. Is this one huge monster?
Three small monsters? Or something else?

Several movie films show something
moving in the loch and throwing out
a V-shaped wave, or wake. Two films
were studied by British military photo
experts. They said each showed a large
object moving at speeds of up to 10 miles
an hour. They said it was most likely
a living creature 6 feet wide and 5 feet high.
The drawings shown here are based on
one of these films.

Then there are the sonar findings.

A sonar set is sometimes called an echo-sounder. It sends out bursts of sound underwater. If the sounds strike something, they bounce back, or echo. The echoes are picked up by the sonar set. It changes them into shapes that can be seen on a screen.

Boats sometimes use sonar in Loch Ness. The crews may be checking the water's depth or looking for fish. Some have picked up echoes they didn't expect. The echoes showed a large object that was moving deep down in the loch.

A few scientists have made sonar searches of the loch. They too have found large objects moving as fast as 17 miles an hour. Sometimes there are several of these objects together. They

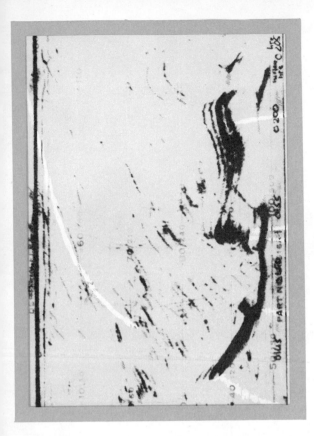

This is a sonar printout,
a record of what showed
on the screen. It seems to show
a school of fish
(small marks at left)
swimming away
from two or more
large moving objects
(big marks at right).

seem to spend their time on the bottom and along the sides of the loch.

Other scientists have taken underwater photos. These are hard to take. The waters of Loch Ness are dark and cloudy. A strong light reaches only a few feet. Even so, the cameras did catch something.

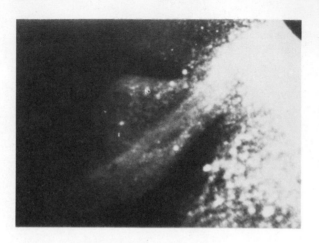

This underwater photo
was taken in August 1972 by a team
headed by Dr. Robert H. Rines
of the Academy of Applied Science.
It seems to show the flipper and side
of a large animal. The flipper
is 6 to 8 feet long and
2 to 4 feet wide. No known animal
of today has a flipper
of this shape.

This photo seems to be of a head. Some people think this is not the monster but something else, perhaps the head of a dead deer.

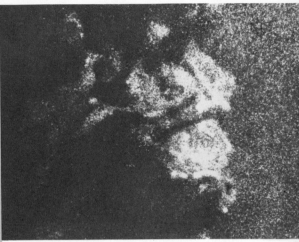

In June 1975 the same team took these underwater photos in Urquhart Bay. This one seems to show the body of an animal with a long neck gliding toward the camera. Is it really an animal? Or is it, as some people think, a cloud of bubbles?

Drawing shows what artist saw in photo.

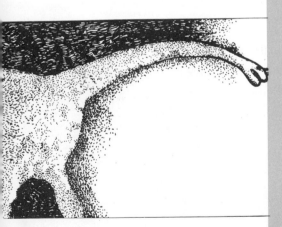

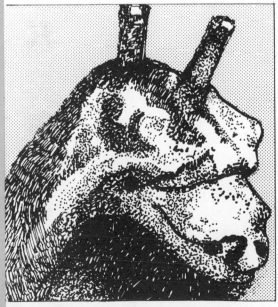

Drawing shows what artist saw in photo above.

Pictures and sonar findings have caused some scientists to take a fresh look at Loch Ness. They now think that the monster is not a joke after all. In fact, they think there is a whole colony of big, strange animals in Loch Ness.

The monster at last? No, this is a dummy made for a movie that was being filmed in Urquhart Bay. The dummy broke away, sank, and is still in the bay.

2. Where Did They Come From?

Where could monsters have come from? The most likely answer is that they came from the sea. They were sea creatures that became trapped in the loch.

There are two ways this could have happened. One has to do with the Ice Age.

The Ice Age began about a million years ago, and it had four stages. Four times, huge sheets of ice spread over large parts of the earth. Four times the ice melted and sent floods of water into the seas.

During the fourth stage, a long tongue of ice flowed northeast in Scotland. Its leading edge was like the blade of a giant bulldozer. All things gave way before it. The ice ripped up land and carved its way through rock. It made a deep U-shaped cut in the earth. Today that cut is the bed of Loch Ness.

About 18,000 years ago, the ice started to melt again. Sea levels began rising. The seas reached inland and flooded valleys and other low-lying areas. Loch Ness was then an arm of the sea.

By 10,000 years ago, Scotland was free of ice. Perhaps it was then that some huge sea creatures arrived. They found their way into sheltered waters. They made their home in an arm of the sea.

But a change was taking place. For thousands of years, Scotland had been buried under ice a mile thick. This great weight had forced the land down into the earth. Now that the ice was gone, Scotland very slowly began to rise. The arm of the sea also rose, for it was really part of the land. In time, it became a lake—Loch Ness, which today is 52 feet above sea level.

The huge creatures were trapped. They could no longer return to the sea. The only way out was through the River Ness. And it was too shallow for them.

In the beginning, Loch Ness was

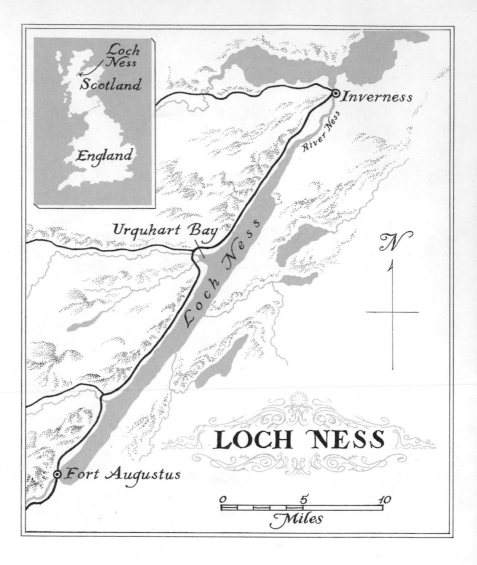

filled with seawater. But freshwater rivers were flowing into it. Over many years, the loch changed. Perhaps the monsters could live in either fresh water or salt. Or perhaps their bodies were able to change. Somehow they were able to go on living in the loch.

If this idea is right, monsters have been living in Loch Ness for several thousand years. This means they must be breeding. There must be males and females. The females must be laying eggs or giving birth to young.

But suppose that no monsters were trapped when the loch rose. How else could they have got in?

Perhaps young monsters came from the sea and swam up the River Ness. That is how salmon, sea trout, and young eels get into the loch. While living in the loch, the young monsters grew into huge adults. The adults were trapped. They were too big to get out through the River Ness.

Perhaps this happened only once, and that was how a colony formed. Or perhaps it is still happening. If so, this might explain something interesting. There have been reports of monsters in other lakes. All of these lakes are also linked to the sea. The same thing could be happening in them. Some are too small to have colonies of monsters, but they could have one that swam in when it was young and grew too big to get out.

Loch Ness is big enough for several large monsters and a number of smaller ones. But monsters would need more than space. They would, for example, need a large food supply. Does Loch Ness have that food? What kind of a home is it? The answers offer some clues to what the monsters might be.

3. The Loch as a Home

Loch Ness is a chilly home. Water near the surface warms up in summer. But the deep water is cold all year round. It is about ten degrees above freezing. The loch can be a home only for animals that do well in cold water.

The loch is also a freshwater home. It is fed by a number of small rivers and streams. Many of these run through peat bogs on their way to the loch. Peat is the remains of ancient plant matter. The running water picks up tiny pieces of peat and carries them along into the loch. The peat makes the loch slightly acid.

The cold, slightly acid water may explain something that is puzzling. If there have been monsters in the loch for hundreds of years, some must have died. Where are the bodies? Why has no one ever seen the body of a dead monster floating in the loch?

In a different kind of lake, a dead body is likely to fill with gas and rise. The gas forms as tiny living things feed on the flesh. These tiny things are bacteria, and they cause dead matter to rot. But in cold, acid water, bacteria are not very active. Their feeding is slow. The gas escapes instead of building up, and the body

Ruins of a castle overlook Urquhart Bay in Loch Ness.

does not rise. The remains of monsters may be on the bottom of the loch.

The tiny pieces of peat also make the water cloudy. Light passes through it only to a depth of about 50 feet. With so little light, there is not much plant life in the loch.

This means the monsters cannot be plant eaters. If there are monsters, they must be fish eaters. There are plenty of fish in the loch.

Brown trout, arctic char, and pike live in the loch all year round. Large numbers of other fishes come and go. Among them are sea trout, salmon, and eels.

Young eels come from the sea and live in the loch for years. They return to the sea when they are ready to spawn, or shed their eggs.

Salmon and sea trout are fishes that hatch out in freshwater streams. They live in fresh water until they are big enough to go to sea. They spend years at sea but return to spawn in fresh water.

Every spawning season, millions of big salmon enter Loch Ness. Each is heading for the stream in which it hatched out. But the salmon must wait in the loch for the right moment. The streams are fed by rain. If there has been little rain, the streams may be too low for the salmon to swim up. If there have been heavy rains, the water may be flowing too fast. Sometimes the salmon must wait for weeks before they can swim to their spawning grounds.

Atlantic salmon do not die after

spawning, as Pacific salmon do. Instead, they go back to sea. After spawning, millions of big salmon again pass through Loch Ness.

Even when they are gone, there are still salmon in the loch. These are young salmon that have hatched out and moved downstream. They live in the loch until they are two years old. Then they are ready to go to sea.

Loch Ness has huge numbers of fish all year round. If it also has monsters, they must be fish eaters that are at home in cold, fresh water.

What kind of animals could these be?

4. What Could They Be?

The animal kingdom is big. It takes in everything from elephants and dinosaurs to hummingbirds and fleas. Within the kingdom, scientists arrange animals in groups. They are groups of like kinds. For example, one big group is called the mammals. It takes in all the animals that nurse their young on milk. Each group takes in animals that are alive today. It also takes in kinds that have died out. Usually these animals are known from their fossils. Fossils are remains preserved in rock.

The mystery monsters must be part of the animal kingdom. They could be a kind of animal we know today. They could be a kind we don't know of at all. They could even be a kind thought to have died out—but still alive. But they must belong to some group.

This early fish, a coelacanth, was thought to have died out 70 million years ago. When fishermen caught two, scientists learned that the fish is still alive today.

In 1958 Francis J. Tully found this fossil
50 miles south of Chicago, in an area where coal
was being mined. It was the fossil of an animal
unlike any known to science. The animal had
a wormlike body with no bones. It had
a long, slim neck and a small head,
a body shaped like a submarine, and a powerful
tail. Its jaws were studded with teeth.
It was named Tully's monster, after its discoverer.

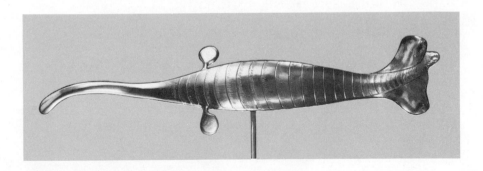

Model of Tully's monster was based on fossils.
It looks rather like a plesiosaur, except for
the strange bar across its chest. It also fits
descriptions of the Loch Ness monster, except
for one thing. It is only a few inches long.

What could they be? One way to attack the mystery is to look at the most likely animal groups. Which of their members could live in Loch Ness? Do the same animals match the accounts of the monsters?

Mammals?

Most kinds of mammals live on land. But some live in the water. Among these are whales, seals, and sea cows. Could any of these be the mystery monsters?

Whales are big enough. They are excellent swimmers and divers. They can live in cold water. And the toothed whales are fish eaters. But otherwise they do not seem likely. They are the wrong shape—no whale has a long neck and a small head. No whale can climb out of the water. And whales are often seen at the surface. Like all mammals, they breathe air through lungs. They must surface to breathe.

Seals are also excellent swimmers and divers that eat fish and are at home in cold water. They are a better shape than whales. But they don't seem very likely either. Seals come ashore too often. They sun themselves out of the water. Their pups are born on land. Some kinds come ashore to sleep. If the monsters were seals, there would be no mystery.

The sea cows of today grow only 8 to 12 feet long. They have short necks. They live in warm, shallow waters. They are plant eaters. And they cannot climb out of the water.

Giant sea cows used to live in cold, shallow waters.

Today's sea cows are much smaller. They are plant eaters that live in warm, shallow waters.

These sea cows seem even more unlikely than whales and seals. But there used to be other, bigger sea cows.

Big sea cows lived in cold water in many parts of the world. We know about them mostly from their fossils. But one group was still living in the North Pacific Ocean in 1741. These are called Steller's sea cows after the scientist who studied them. We know about them only from his notes. Thirty years after Steller studied them, they were gone. They had been wiped out by Russian hunters.

Steller's sea cows grew 25 to 30 feet long and weighed more than four tons. Their heads were small. In deep water these animals often floated with their heads and tails hanging down and their backs arched. To Steller, a float-ing sea cow looked like an overturned boat.

Steller's sea cow had a hump at the shoulder. When a mother carried her calf on her back, she appeared to have two humps.

These sea cows were hard to see from a distance. Their bodies were usually underwater, and so were their heads. But every four or five minutes they lifted their nostrils out of the water to snort and breathe.

And that is one problem. Big sea cows might look like the monsters. But they would have to act like mammals. They would have to breathe air. The monsters seem to spend more time un-derwater than any known mammal could.

Then, too, all known sea cows were plant eaters. They all lived in shallow waters. And none could leave the water.

Reptiles?

A turtle has a long neck and a small head. It swims and dives well. Its arched shell might look like an overturned boat. Three turtles swimming together might look like a huge animal with three humps.

Some turtles live in fresh water. They can eat fish, along with many other things. And turtles can leave the water. In fact, sometimes they must leave the water. All turtles mate on land and lay their eggs on land.

Could the Loch Ness monsters be turtles?

A leatherback is the largest known turtle.

Size is one problem. The largest known turtle grows about 10 feet long. This is a sea turtle called the leatherback. No one really knows if a turtle could grow any bigger. Turtles do most of their growing in their first 10 years. After that they do go on growing, but very slowly. However, they may live a long time—100 years or more.

Another problem is that turtles are air breathers. Turtles belong to the group of animals called reptiles. Crocodiles, snakes, and lizards are also reptiles. Like mammals, all reptiles breathe air through lungs. Turtles must surface to breathe.

A third problem is temperature. Loch Ness is cold for reptiles. Unlike mammals, reptiles do not have bodies that make heat. They take their heat from their surroundings. And they are most active in warm temperatures.

Still, leatherbacks have a way of keeping warm in cold water. They can warm themselves by swimming actively. They can make heat by using their muscles. But to do this, a leatherback must breathe often. It must raise its head out of the water two or three times ·a minute. It is easily seen.

There is one other reptile that might live in Loch Ness. It was a relative of the dinosaurs, called a plesiosaur. Plesiosaurs were big reptiles that lived in warm, shallow seas. In all, there were about 30 kinds of plesiosaur. Two or three sound like the Loch Ness monsters.

These plesiosaurs grew to a length of about 20 feet. Each had a long neck with a small head, flippers, and a thick body with a humped back. The teeth show that they were fish eaters. When chasing fish, they sometimes swam up rivers into fresh water.

Could there possibly be plesiosaurs in Loch Ness?

46

Drawing shows one kind of Plesiosaurus at left.
Giant reptile chasing fish is a relative.
It is one kind of Thaumatosaurus.

One problem is that plesiosaurs seem to have died out 65 million years ago, along with the dinosaurs.

But suppose they didn't. Suppose they were able to go on living in warm, shallow seas. Suppose they were still there when the fourth stage of the Ice Age ended. Why did they then swim north to the deep, cold waters off Scotland?

Once there, could they have lived year round in cold water? No one knows for sure, but it is just possible.

Dinosaurs have always been classed as reptiles. But some scientists now think they were not true reptiles. They think the bodies of dinosaurs could make and hold heat. Perhaps this was also true of the plesiosaurs.

However, there is still one other big problem. All plesiosaurs breathed air through lungs. If there are plesiosaurs in Loch Ness, they should often be at or near the surface.

5. What Else Could They Be?

Amphibians?

Frogs, toads, and salamanders belong to the group of animals called amphibians. Most amphibians spend one part of their life in water. They spend another part on land. This double life accounts for their name. It comes from two Greek words, *amphi,* meaning "two," and *bios,* meaning "life."

Could the Loch Ness monsters be giant amphibians?

Frogs and toads are the wrong shape. But salamanders are more or less the right shape. A salamander has a long body and a long tail.

Salamanders could live in Loch Ness. They do well in cool places. If they live in water, they live only in fresh water. Salamanders eat almost anything that moves. The loch's fishes would be their food supply.

The monster is sometimes said to have a stiff mane or fin. Nearly all young salamanders have a frilly fin on the back. Some adults also have this fin.

The monster is sometimes said to have horns or feelers. No salamander has these. But some salamanders have something that might look like horns. They have gills on the outside of the body. The gills branch out behind the head.

The monster seems able to breathe both in water and in air. A salamander is one of the few animals that might also be able to do this. Among salamanders there are three ways of breathing.

One is with gills. Young salamanders that hatch out in water have gills. They take oxygen from the water through their gills.

The second is with lungs. As young salamanders grow up, many kinds lose their gills. They develop lungs. Most of these leave the water.

The third way of breathing is through the skin. A salamander that breathes this way may or may not have gills.

Young tiger salamander (above) has gills
that branch out behind head.

Adult (below) has lost its gills
and developed lungs.

Perhaps the Loch Ness monster is a kind of salamander we don't know. It might have gills and a partly developed lung. It might also be able to breathe through its skin. If so, it could spend long periods underwater. It could also breathe at the surface and on land.

But in other ways, salamanders seem less likely to be the monsters.

Salamanders have short necks and big heads.

Most of today's salamanders are small. To find big salamanders, we have to go far back in time—150 to 270 million years. In those days there were 15-foot-long salamanders. Fossils of some have been found in Scotland.

But in those millions of years, many great changes have taken place on earth. A recent one was the Ice Age. Suppose there were giant salamanders in Scotland when the Ice Age began. What became of them? They could not have lived on land. But salamanders cannot live in salt water. So they could not have escaped into the sea.

Where could they have come from when Loch Ness became a freshwater lake?

Fish?

An eel looks like a snake, but it is not a reptile. It is a bony fish—an animal with a backbone that lives in water and breathes through gills. Many kinds of eels can live only in salt water. But there are also freshwater eels that spend most of their lives in lakes, ponds, and streams.

Of all fishes, eels are most likely to be the monsters of Loch Ness. There are many things about eels that seem just right.

Eels can—and do—live in the cold, fresh water of Loch Ness. And there is plenty of food for them. An eel's jaws are lined with sharp teeth. It feeds on other animals, both dead and alive.

An eel has no neck. But sometimes an eel pokes it head and part of its body out of the water. Then it looks as if it had a long neck and a small head.

An eel does not have flippers. But it has something that might look like them. It has two fins on the front part of its body.

It has a long back fin that looks

something like a frill. This fin could easily be taken for a mane. It looks even more like a mane when an eel sticks its tail out of the water.

Eels swim with a snakelike motion, moving their bodies from side to side. Seen from a distance, a swimming eel looks as if it had humps. If it swims

A giant eel might seem to have humps, a mane, a long neck and a small head, and flippers.

on its side then it really does have humps. Eels are fast swimmers. They can both dive and sink from sight.

Sometimes eels come to the surface to hunt. An eel may lie in wait and grab a fish as it swims by. Or it may track a fish.

It is also true that eels are able to leave the water. On land they breathe through their moist skins.

In all these ways, eels seem as if they might be the monsters of Loch Ness. But there are problems with eels, too.

One is size. Freshwater eels usually grow only five or six feet long. Perhaps they could grow much bigger, but they do not seem to have time. Most die when they are quite young.

This is what happens. The eels

found inland are usually females. When they are 5 to 12 years old, their skin color darkens. This is a sign that they are getting ready to spawn. They can spawn only in salt water.

To reach the sea, some females need only swim down a river. Others have to travel over land. They may do this to reach a river that runs to the sea. Or they may need to get around a dam.

Males live where rivers meet the sea. The females join them, and all begin a long journey to the place where they were born. They swim far out into the Atlantic Ocean. There the eels spawn and die.

Millions of tiny eel eggs float and drift, then hatch out into tiny creatures. Currents carry the young back to the shores and rivers from which the adults came.

If there are monster eels in Loch Ness, some females must have simply stayed there. Perhaps from time to time there is a female that never becomes ready to spawn. So she never leaves for the sea. In this case she might grow very big.

Most fishes keep growing for as long as they live. Their growth may slow, but it never stops. A fish that lives a long time can grow very big.

Fishes may die for a number of reasons. But if nothing harms a fish, scientists think it could live a very long time. Fishes age more slowly than mammals.

But could an eel grow to monster size? No one knows.

Mollusks?

To some people the monster has looked like a huge slug or a snail without a shell. The slugs we know best are those found in gardens. But there are other kinds in the sea.

Slugs belong to a very big group of animals called mollusks. Mollusks are among the animals without backbones. They have rubbery bodies with no bones. The most familiar mollusks are clams, oysters, mussels, octopuses, snails, and slugs. Of them all, slugs sound most like the monsters.

A slug can stretch its body out long. It can pull its body together. The same slug might look 50 feet long in one sighting and 20 feet long in another. Pulled together, the back might look like an overturned boat.

Some people say the monster looks like a giant garden slug. Garden slugs cannot live in water.

But other kinds of slugs, such as this one, can and do live in water.

Sea slugs do not have fins or flippers. But some kinds have rounded paddles, with which they row. Some kinds have bristles, which might look like a mane. They have growths on the head that might look like feelers.

A few kinds of slugs can breathe both in water and in air.

Giant sea slugs could live in the cold water of Loch Ness. Some kinds would do well feeding on fish. But no sea slug known today can live in fresh water.

A much bigger problem has to do with bones. In other types of animals, bones are the framework of the body. They support the muscles and flesh. A slug's body has no such support.

The monster is said to stick a 6-foot-long neck out of the water. Could an animal without bones hold up such a long neck? It does not seem likely.

A giant slug could easily live in water. The water would buoy up the body, and the slug would be weight-less. But a giant slug could not leave the water. On land, it might weigh a ton or more. Without bones, it would be crushed under its own very great weight.

Several animals seem as if they might be the mystery monsters of Loch Ness. But no one fits perfectly. Each kind has certain problems. That is why the mystery goes on.

As this book was written, scientists were still trying to solve the mystery of Loch Ness. Perhaps they will, but perhaps they won't. It is, after all, a very old mystery.

But you have now read the evidence. You have seen the clues. What do you think about the mystery monsters of Loch Ness?

INDEX

Amphibians, 49-51, 53-54

Coelacanth, 36 (pic)

Dinosaurs, 47 , 48

Eels, 56 (pic)
    appearance, 55
    breathing, 57
    growth, 59
    life span, 59
    movement, 56
    reproduction, 58-59
    size, 57

Fish, 54-59
Fossils, 35

Ice Age, 23-24, 48, 54

Loch Ness, 26 (map), 31 (pic)
    acidity, 30
    bacteria, 30
    description, 7
    fish in, 32-34
    origin, 24-25
    peat in, 29-30, 32
    plant life, 32
    size, 28
    temperature, 29
Loch Ness monster
    first newspaper account of, 10
    naming of, 10
    photographs of, 14, 15-16 (pics), 20-21 (pics)
    possible origins of, 25, 27
    sightings of, 12 (pic), 14
    sonar findings, 18, 19 (pic)

Mammals, 38-39, 41-43
Mollusks, 60-63

Plesiosaurs, 47 (pic)
    body temperature, 48
    breathing, 48
    diet, 46
    size, 46
    where they lived, 46

Reptiles, 43-48
River Ness, 25, 27

Salamanders, 52 (pic)
    appearance, 50, 53
    breathing, 51, 53
    diet, 50
    fossils, 53
    size, 53
Salmon, 33-34
Scotland, 7, 24-25, 54
    and Ice Age, 24-25
Sea Cows
    present-day, 39, 40 (pic)
    Steller's sea cow, 40 (pic), 41-43
Seals, 39
Slugs, 61 (pics)
    characteristics of, 61
    diet, 62
    structure, 63

Tully's monster, 37 (pic)
Turtles, 44 (pic)
    breathing, 45-46
    diet, 43
    life span, 45
    movement, 43
    reproduction, 43
    size, 44

Whales, 38